Structured Couture Creatir
Designs with Precision

Bruce Fred

Copyright © [2023]

Title: Structured Couture Creating High-Fashion Designs with Precision
Author's: Bruce Fred

This book was printed and published by [Publisher's: **Bruce Fred**] in [2023]

ISBN:

TABLE OF CONTENT

Chapter 1: Introduction to Structured Design in Fashion

Understanding the Importance of Structure in Fashion Design

In the world of fashion design, structure plays a crucial role in creating stunning and high-fashion designs. From perfectly tailored garments to architectural silhouettes, understanding the importance of structure is essential for any fashion designer, especially those specializing in structured design. This subchapter will delve into the significance of structure in fashion design, providing valuable insights for aspiring fashion designers.

Structure in fashion design refers to the framework, foundation, and overall construction of a garment. It involves various elements, such as pattern making, cut, fabric choice, and construction techniques, which work together to create visually appealing and well-fitting designs. Whether it's a structured jacket, a tailored dress, or a voluminous skirt, the right structure is what sets these designs apart from the rest.

One of the key reasons why structure is vital in fashion design is its ability to enhance the overall aesthetic appeal of a garment. A well-structured design can elevate a simple outfit to a high-fashion statement. It adds dimension, shape, and form, creating visually striking silhouettes that catch the eye and leave a lasting impression. By understanding the principles of structured design, fashion designers can create unique and innovative pieces that stand out in the competitive fashion industry.

Additionally, structure plays a significant role in ensuring the perfect fit of a garment. A well-structured design provides support, shape, and comfort to the wearer. By utilizing precise pattern making techniques, designers can create garments that flatter the body and accentuate the wearer's best features. Understanding how structure interacts with different body types and proportions is crucial in achieving the desired fit and creating designs that make individuals feel confident and beautiful.

Furthermore, structure enables designers to experiment with unconventional materials and push the boundaries of fashion. By incorporating architectural elements, unconventional patterns, and innovative construction techniques, fashion designers can create unique and boundary-pushing designs. The use of structure allows for the creation of avant-garde fashion pieces that challenge traditional norms and inspire creativity within the industry.

In conclusion, understanding the importance of structure in fashion design is essential for any aspiring fashion designer, particularly those specializing in structured design. Structure not only enhances the aesthetic appeal of a garment but also ensures the perfect fit and enables experimentation with unconventional materials. By mastering the principles of structured design, fashion designers can create high-fashion designs that captivate the audience and establish their unique artistic vision within the fashion industry.

The Evolution of Structured Couture

In the ever-changing landscape of fashion design, one aspect that has consistently captivated both designers and fashion enthusiasts alike is the evolution of structured couture. This subchapter delves into the fascinating journey of structured design for fashion, tracing its origins, significant milestones, and the impact it has had on the industry.

Structured couture, with its emphasis on precision and meticulous construction, has long been an integral part of high-fashion designs. Its roots can be traced back to the early 20th century when designers began experimenting with new techniques and materials to create garments that defied convention. One of the pioneers in this field was Paul Poiret, who introduced the concept of corsetless dresses, liberating women from the restrictive undergarments of the time.

The 1940s and 1950s witnessed a further evolution of structured couture, with designers such as Christian Dior and Cristóbal Balenciaga leading the way. Dior's "New Look" featured cinched waists and exaggerated hips, while Balenciaga's architectural silhouettes showcased his mastery of draping and construction. These designers pushed the boundaries of structure, employing innovative techniques and experimenting with new fabrics to create garments that were both visually striking and wearable.

The 1960s and 1970s saw a shift in structured couture, with designers like Pierre Cardin and André Courrèges embracing futuristic elements and geometric shapes. Their designs incorporated bold lines and sharp angles, challenging traditional notions of structure and pushing the boundaries of what was considered fashionable.

In recent decades, structured couture has continued to evolve, with designers like Alexander McQueen, Iris van Herpen, and Gareth Pugh pushing the limits of construction and incorporating technology into their designs. 3D printing, laser cutting, and other innovative techniques have allowed them to create garments that were once unimaginable, blurring the line between fashion and art.

The impact of structured design for fashion cannot be overstated. It has not only influenced the way garments are constructed but also how they are perceived. Structured couture has the power to transform a simple piece of fabric into a work of art, elevating fashion to a form of self-expression and storytelling.

For aspiring fashion designers interested in structured design, this subchapter serves as a comprehensive exploration of its evolution. By understanding the historical context and the groundbreaking contributions of past designers, one can gain inspiration and insights to create their own unique, structured couture designs. The journey of structured couture continues to unfold, and it is an exciting time for those passionate about pushing the boundaries of fashion and creating designs that captivate and inspire.

Overview of High-Fashion Designs with Precision

When it comes to fashion design, precision is key. In the world of structured design for fashion, attention to detail and meticulous craftsmanship are what set high-fashion creations apart from the rest. In this subchapter titled "Overview of High-Fashion Designs with Precision," we will delve into the fundamental aspects of creating exquisite structured couture.

Structured couture is a discipline that demands a deep understanding of construction techniques and a keen eye for precision. It involves the art of creating garments that exhibit architectural elements, impeccable tailoring, and a flawless fit. The result is a stunning ensemble that exudes sophistication, elegance, and originality.

To achieve this level of perfection, fashion designers must start with a strong foundation of knowledge and skills. The subchapter will explore the various elements that contribute to the creation of high-fashion designs with precision. We will dive into topics such as fabric selection, pattern making, draping, and the importance of proper measurements.

Fabric selection plays a crucial role in structured couture. The choice of fabric can greatly impact the overall look and feel of a garment. We will discuss the different types of fabrics commonly used in structured designs, their properties, and how to make informed decisions when selecting the most appropriate fabric for a specific design.

Pattern making and draping are essential techniques in structured couture. Our subchapter will provide an introduction to these techniques, explaining their significance in achieving precision and structure in high-fashion designs. We will explore the principles behind pattern making and draping, discussing how to manipulate fabric and create three-dimensional shapes that accentuate the body's natural curves.

Additionally, we will emphasize the importance of taking accurate measurements. Precision in measurements ensures that the final garment fits the wearer perfectly, enhancing their confidence and comfort. We will guide fashion designers on how to take precise measurements and translate them into well-fitting patterns.

Ultimately, this subchapter aims to equip aspiring fashion designers with a comprehensive overview of high-fashion designs with precision. By understanding the intricate details of fabric selection, pattern making, draping, and measurements, they will be able to create structured couture that captivates audiences and pushes the boundaries of fashion design. With this knowledge, they will embark on a journey of crafting unique and breathtaking fashion creations that leave a lasting impression in the world of high fashion.

Chapter 2: Fundamentals of Structured Design

Principles of Structural Design in Fashion

In the fast-paced world of fashion design, creating high-fashion designs that stand out from the crowd requires precision and attention to detail. One niche that has gained increasing popularity is structured design for fashion. This subchapter aims to explore the principles of structural design in fashion, providing valuable insights and guidance for fashion designers looking to incorporate this technique into their creations.

Structural design in fashion involves using architectural elements and techniques to create garments that possess a strong and defined silhouette. It is about constructing garments that are not only visually striking but also possess a sense of stability and balance. By understanding and applying the principles of structural design, fashion designers can create unique and memorable pieces that push the boundaries of traditional fashion.

One fundamental principle of structural design in fashion is the importance of strong and stable foundations. Just as a building needs a solid base, garments with structural elements require a stable foundation to maintain their shape. This can be achieved through the use of sturdy materials, such as boning or interfacing, which provide support and structure to the garment.

Another key principle is the use of architectural lines and shapes. Structured design often involves incorporating clean lines, geometric shapes, and architectural details into garments. These elements not only add visual interest but also help to create a sense of order and precision in the design. Fashion designers can experiment with various shapes, such as sharp angles, curves, or even asymmetrical lines, to create unique and dynamic structural designs.

Furthermore, the principle of balance plays a crucial role in structural design for fashion. Balancing the weight and volume of the garment is essential to ensure that it doesn't overwhelm the wearer or appear disproportionate. Additionally, considering the balance of the design as a whole, including the placement of structural elements and the flow of the fabric, is crucial to create a harmonious and visually pleasing composition.

Lastly, attention to detail is key in achieving successful structural designs. Precision in construction, such as precise stitching, careful fabric selection, and meticulous finishing techniques, all contribute to the overall quality and durability of the garment. Fashion designers should also pay close attention to fit, ensuring that the structural elements do not hinder the wearer's movement or comfort.

In conclusion, the principles of structural design in fashion offer a framework for fashion designers to create high-fashion designs with precision and impact. By understanding and applying these principles, designers can elevate their creations to new heights, pushing the boundaries of traditional fashion and captivate the audience with unique and memorable structural designs.

Materials and Fabrics for Structured Couture

When it comes to creating high-fashion designs with precision, the choice of materials and fabrics is crucial. In the world of structured couture, where every detail matters, selecting the right materials can make all the difference in achieving impeccable results.

One of the key considerations in structured design for fashion is the stability and durability of the chosen materials. Structured garments require fabrics that can hold their shape and provide support to the overall structure. Stiff fabrics like silk organza, duchess satin, or neoprene are often favored for their ability to maintain a crisp silhouette and provide the desired level of rigidity.

For intricate and complex designs, interfacings and linings play a vital role in providing additional support and structure to the garment. By carefully selecting appropriate interfacings and linings, fashion designers can ensure that their creations maintain their shape and structure over time.

Another essential element in structured couture is the use of embellishments and trims. These elements can enhance the overall aesthetic and add depth to the design. Beads, sequins, lace appliques, and metallic trims are commonly used to create stunning visual effects and highlight specific areas of the garment.

In terms of color palette, structured couture often leans towards bold and vibrant hues. However, neutral tones can also be used to create a timeless and elegant look. The choice of colors should be made in consideration of the overall design concept and the desired impact on the audience.

When it comes to sourcing materials for structured couture, it is important to consider the quality and origin of the fabrics. High-quality materials not only ensure a superior finish but also contribute to sustainable and ethical fashion practices. Opting for fabrics that are responsibly sourced and produced can help promote a more eco-conscious approach to fashion design.

In conclusion, materials and fabrics play a pivotal role in achieving precision and finesse in structured couture. The selection of stable and durable fabrics, along with appropriate interfacings and linings, ensures that the garment maintains its shape and structure. Embellishments and trims add a touch of glamour and sophistication, while the color palette sets the mood and tone of the design. By choosing high-quality and responsibly sourced materials, fashion designers can create structured couture that not only captivates the audience but also promotes sustainability in the industry.

Tools and Techniques for Precision in Fashion Design

Subchapter: Tools and Techniques for Precision in Fashion Design

Precision is the cornerstone of structured design in the world of fashion. From creating perfectly tailored garments to beautifully constructed silhouettes, the use of the right tools and techniques is essential for fashion designers looking to achieve a flawless, high-fashion aesthetic. In this subchapter, we will explore a range of tools and techniques that can elevate your fashion design skills and help you create structured couture with precision.

1. Measuring tools: Accurate measurements are crucial for precise garment construction. Invest in high-quality measuring tapes, rulers, and curved rulers to ensure consistent and precise measurements. These tools will help you create patterns that fit impeccably and achieve clean lines in your designs.

2. Pattern-making tools: Pattern-making is an intricate process that requires precision. Utilize tools like French curves, hip curves, and grading rulers to create seamless patterns with accurate curves and angles. These tools will assist you in achieving the desired fit, shape, and structure in your garments.

3. Cutting tools: Clean and precise cutting is essential for structured designs. Invest in sharp fabric shears, rotary cutters, and dressmaker's scissors to ensure accurate and smooth cutting of various fabrics. These tools will help you achieve clean edges and smooth lines in your designs.

4. Sewing machines: A reliable sewing machine is a designer's best friend. Choose a machine that offers a variety of stitch options and adjustable settings, allowing you to sew different fabric weights and

achieve precise stitching. Explore features like needle position control, automatic tension, and buttonhole options to enhance precision in your sewing.

5. Pressing tools: Proper pressing techniques can transform a garment from average to exceptional. Invest in a high-quality iron, a pressing cloth, and a tailor's ham to achieve crisp seams, sharp pleats, and perfectly pressed darts. These tools will ensure that every detail of your design looks polished and professional.

6. Hand-sewing tools: Hand-sewing techniques are often necessary in structured design. Essential hand-sewing tools include needles, thimbles, embroidery scissors, and a seam ripper. These tools will assist you in achieving precise and invisible stitches, as well as in correcting any mistakes or alterations in your designs.

7. Draping techniques: Draping is a versatile technique used in structured design. Learn the art of draping fabric on a dress form to create unique silhouettes and explore the possibilities of three-dimensional design. Draping allows you to experiment with shape and structure before transferring your ideas to patterns.

By incorporating these tools and techniques into your fashion design practice, you will be able to achieve precise and structured couture. Embrace the art of precision in your creations and watch as your designs elevate to new heights in the world of high fashion.

Chapter 3: Creating Structured Silhouettes

Exploring Different Silhouette Styles

In the world of fashion design, one of the most essential aspects is understanding and experimenting with different silhouette styles. Silhouettes play a crucial role in defining the overall look and feel of a garment, making it imperative for fashion designers to have a deep understanding of this concept. In this subchapter, we will delve into the fascinating world of exploring various silhouette styles, focusing specifically on structured design for fashion design.

Structured design is a niche within the fashion industry that encompasses the creation of high-fashion designs with precision. It involves meticulous attention to detail, impeccable construction techniques, and a keen eye for creating garments that exude elegance and sophistication. To achieve this, designers must have a solid understanding of different silhouette styles and how they can be incorporated into their creations.

The first step in exploring silhouette styles is to understand the basics. Silhouette refers to the outline or shape of a garment, which is determined by the way it hangs on the body. Different silhouettes can evoke various moods and convey different messages. From the classic hourglass shape to the avant-garde asymmetrical designs, each silhouette has its unique charm and appeal.

In this subchapter, we will explore a range of silhouette styles commonly used in structured design for fashion. We will discuss the characteristics of each silhouette, including their proportions, lines, and shapes. From the structured and tailored silhouettes of the 1940s to the voluminous and exaggerated shapes of the 1980s, we will journey through the history of fashion to gain inspiration and insights.

Additionally, we will delve into the techniques and construction methods required to create each silhouette. From pattern making to draping, we will examine the intricate processes involved in bringing these designs to life. This subchapter will serve as a comprehensive guide for fashion designers who wish to master the art of structured design and create high-fashion garments with precision.

By exploring different silhouette styles, fashion designers can expand their creative horizons and develop their unique design aesthetic. Whether they choose to embrace the timeless elegance of a tailored silhouette or experiment with bold and unconventional shapes, understanding the nuances of silhouettes is paramount to achieving success in the world of structured fashion design.

In conclusion, this subchapter, "Exploring Different Silhouette Styles," is an essential resource for fashion designers who specialize in structured design. By delving into the history, characteristics, and construction techniques associated with various silhouette styles, designers can enhance their skills and create high-fashion garments with precision. With the knowledge gained from this subchapter, fashion designers will be well-equipped to push the boundaries of structured design and create stunning, innovative designs that captivate the fashion industry.

Drafting Patterns for Structured Bodices

In the world of fashion design, creating structured bodices that exude elegance and sophistication requires precision and attention to detail. In this subchapter of "Structured Couture: Creating High-Fashion Designs with Precision," we delve into the art of drafting patterns for structured bodices, providing invaluable insights and techniques for fashion designers who specialize in structured design.

A structured bodice serves as the foundation for any garment, providing the necessary support and shape that defines the overall silhouette. To achieve this, it is crucial to understand the principles of pattern drafting and how they can be adapted to create a structured design.

This subchapter begins by exploring the key elements of a structured bodice, such as darts, seams, and boning channels. We dissect each element, explaining their purpose and how they contribute to the overall structure of the garment. By understanding these fundamental components, fashion designers can experiment with various design possibilities, pushing the boundaries of structured design.

Next, we delve into the process of pattern drafting for structured bodices. We provide step-by-step instructions, accompanied by detailed diagrams and illustrations, on how to measure the body accurately and translate those measurements into a precise pattern. We discuss the importance of fitting toile, a mock-up garment, to ensure the perfect fit and make necessary adjustments before moving on to the final garment.

Throughout this subchapter, we emphasize the significance of precision in structured design. From measuring to cutting fabric, every step requires meticulous attention to detail. We also offer tips and tricks on handling challenging fabrics, such as silk or lace, to achieve the desired structure without compromising the design's integrity.

Moreover, we explore different techniques for constructing structured bodices, such as boning and interlining. We discuss the various types of boning available and how to select the appropriate one for different designs. Additionally, we provide insights into interlining fabrics, their purpose, and how they contribute to the overall structure and shape of the garment.

Whether you are a budding fashion designer or an experienced professional looking to enhance your skills in structured design, this subchapter on drafting patterns for structured bodices is an essential resource. It equips you with the knowledge and techniques needed to create high-fashion designs that exude precision and elegance. Unlock the secrets of structured design and elevate your fashion creations to new heights.

Constructing Structured Skirts and Bottoms

When it comes to creating high-fashion designs with precision, constructing structured skirts and bottoms plays a crucial role in achieving the desired look and fit. This subchapter will delve into the art of designing and crafting these essential elements, catering specifically to the niche of structured design for fashion design.

Structured skirts and bottoms are known for their clean lines, impeccable fit, and architectural silhouette. They add sophistication and elegance to any outfit, making them a staple in high-end fashion. To create these pieces, it is essential to understand the principles of construction, fabric selection, and techniques that contribute to their structured appearance.

One of the primary considerations in constructing structured skirts and bottoms is fabric choice. Fabrics with more body and structure, such as wool, tweed, or heavy-weight cotton, are ideal for achieving the desired shape and form. These fabrics provide stability and ensure that the garment maintains its intended silhouette.

Pattern drafting is a crucial step in creating structured bottoms. Proper measurements and precise calculations are essential to achieve a flawless fit. This subchapter will guide fashion designers through the process of drafting patterns for various skirt and bottom styles, including pencil skirts, A-line skirts, tailored trousers, and culottes.

To enhance the structured appearance, various construction techniques can be employed. These techniques include using interfacing, boning, or horsehair braid to provide shape and support to the garment. Additionally, incorporating darts, pleats, or tucks can add structure and visually interesting details.

The subchapter will also cover the importance of accurate cutting and sewing techniques to ensure clean lines and a professional finish. Sewing methods like understitching, topstitching, and invisible zippers will be explored, enabling fashion designers to achieve expert-level construction.

Lastly, the subchapter will provide inspiration and examples of renowned designers who have mastered the art of constructing structured skirts and bottoms. Examining their work will offer valuable insights into the creative possibilities and potential applications of structured design in the fashion industry.

In conclusion, constructing structured skirts and bottoms is a fundamental skill in the world of high-fashion design. This subchapter caters specifically to fashion designers interested in structured design, providing guidance on fabric selection, pattern drafting, construction techniques, and sewing methods. By mastering these skills, designers will be equipped to create impeccable, architectural silhouettes and elevate their designs to the realm of structured couture.

Designing Structured Sleeves and Collars

In the world of high-fashion design, attention to detail and precision are paramount. Structured sleeves and collars not only add a touch of elegance and sophistication to garments but also serve as powerful design elements that can transform a simple outfit into a work of art. This subchapter will delve into the intricacies of designing structured sleeves and collars, offering insights and techniques that will inspire and guide fashion designers specializing in structured design.

When it comes to sleeves, structure can be achieved through various methods. One popular technique is the use of padding or boning, which adds volume and shape to the sleeves. This method is particularly effective for creating puffed or bishop sleeves that exude drama and grandeur. By strategically placing padding or boning, designers can manipulate the silhouette and create eye-catching dimensions.

Another approach to structured sleeves involves pleating and gathering techniques. These techniques allow designers to create intricate and unique textures while maintaining a tailored look. Pleats can be placed strategically to add fullness or create a sculptural effect, while gathering can be used to create soft drapes or cascades.

In the realm of collars, structure plays a crucial role in defining the neckline and enhancing the overall aesthetic of a garment. Collars can be designed to stand tall and make a bold statement or be more subtle and delicate, depending on the desired effect. Techniques such as interfacing and wire insertion can be employed to achieve the desired shape and stiffness.

When designing structured collars, it is important to consider the garment's neckline and silhouette. A high collar may be more suitable for a tailored jacket, while a softer, draped collar may complement a flowing dress. The choice of fabric is also key in achieving the desired structure and drape. Stiffer fabrics like silk organza or taffeta work well for more structured collars, while softer fabrics like chiffon or silk charmeuse lend themselves to more fluid designs.

Designing structured sleeves and collars requires a meticulous approach and an eye for detail. By incorporating padding, boning, pleating, gathering, and careful fabric selection, fashion designers can create extraordinary pieces that stand out in the world of structured design. The possibilities are endless, and this subchapter serves as a comprehensive guide for fashion designers looking to push the boundaries of structured couture and create high-fashion designs that exude precision and artistry.

Chapter 4: Incorporating Structural Elements in Garments

Working with Corsets and Boning

Corsets have long been a staple in the world of fashion, providing structure and support to garments while enhancing the wearer's figure. In the realm of structured design for fashion, corsets and boning play a crucial role in creating high-fashion designs with precision. This subchapter will delve into the intricacies of working with corsets and boning, offering valuable insights and techniques for fashion designers looking to master this art form.

When it comes to corset construction, selecting the right materials is essential. High-quality fabrics such as coutil, brocade, or silk are often used for the corset's exterior, while a sturdy lining fabric provides reinforcement. Boning, typically made of steel or plastic, is inserted into channels within the corset to provide structure and shape. It is crucial to choose the appropriate boning type and size based on the desired level of support and flexibility.

Understanding the different types of boning is essential for achieving the desired results. Spiral steel boning is flexible and ideal for curved areas like the waistline, while flat steel boning offers more rigidity and is perfect for vertical support. Plastic boning is lightweight and suitable for garments that require less shaping. By strategically combining different types of boning, fashion designers can create corsets that mold to the body while maintaining their structural integrity.

Proper construction techniques are crucial when working with corsets and boning. Designers must learn to sew precise boning channels to ensure the boning stays in place and does not poke through the fabric. Adding a waist tape, a narrow strip of fabric, further reinforces the waistline and provides additional stability to the corset. It is also essential to master techniques such as hand-stitching eyelets, adding busks or lacing, and creating a flawless fit through careful fitting and adjustments.

Working with corsets and boning requires patience, attention to detail, and a deep understanding of garment construction. By mastering these skills, fashion designers can create stunning structured designs that elevate their collections to new heights. Whether it's a striking evening gown or a tailored jacket, the inclusion of corsets and boning can transform a garment into a work of art, highlighting the wearer's silhouette and adding a touch of elegance.

In conclusion, this subchapter on working with corsets and boning provides fashion designers specializing in structured design with invaluable insights and techniques. By understanding the materials, boning types, and construction techniques involved, designers can create exquisite high-fashion designs that epitomize precision and style. With their ability to shape and support the body, corsets and boning are essential tools in the arsenal of any fashion designer looking to make a statement in the world of structured couture.

Adding Structured Panels and Seams

Structured Couture: Creating High-Fashion Designs with Precision

Structuring a garment is a crucial element in creating high-fashion designs that exude sophistication and precision. The use of structured panels and seams adds depth, shape, and architectural interest to garments, elevating them from ordinary to extraordinary. In this subchapter, we will explore the art of incorporating structured panels and seams into fashion designs, allowing you to create unique and visually striking pieces.

When it comes to structured design in fashion, panels and seams play a pivotal role in achieving the desired effect. Panels are separate fabric pieces that are strategically placed on a garment to create shape, volume, or architectural lines. Seams, on the other hand, are the stitching lines that join these panels together. By understanding how to manipulate these elements, you can transform your designs into stunning works of art.

One technique to consider when adding structured panels and seams is the use of contrasting fabrics. Experiment with different textures, colors, and patterns to create visual interest and highlight specific areas of the garment. For example, combining a structured wool panel with a flowy silk one can create a juxtaposition that adds drama and intrigue to the design.

Another technique to explore is the use of geometric shapes. Incorporating triangular, rectangular, or angular panels can create a bold and modern aesthetic. By strategically placing these panels along the garment's contours, you can enhance the wearer's silhouette and create a visually captivating design.

Additionally, consider playing with the placement of seams to create unique and unexpected lines. Experiment with curved or diagonal seams to add movement and fluidity to your designs. These subtle details can make a significant difference in the overall structure and visual appeal of the garment.

To ensure precision and accuracy when adding structured panels and seams, it is crucial to pay attention to the construction process. Carefully measure and mark the fabric, use high-quality materials, and employ precise sewing techniques. Taking the time to perfect these details will result in a flawless finished product.

In conclusion, incorporating structured panels and seams into your fashion designs is a powerful way to elevate them to a high-fashion level. By experimenting with contrasting fabrics, geometric shapes, and seam placement, you can create visually striking and architecturally interesting garments. Remember to focus on precision and accuracy during the construction process to ensure a flawless finish. With these techniques, you will be able to create structured designs that make a statement in the world of fashion.

Creating Sculptural Drapes and Folds

When it comes to structured design in fashion, one technique that can add depth, dimension, and drama to garments is creating sculptural drapes and folds. These architectural elements can transform a simple design into a high-fashion statement piece, capturing attention and leaving a lasting impression.

To achieve sculptural drapes and folds, it is essential to understand the principles of fabric manipulation. By skillfully using pleating, ruching, gathering, and origami-inspired techniques, fashion designers can create stunning visual effects and unique silhouettes.

One of the most commonly used methods for creating sculptural drapes is pleating. Pleats add structure and volume to fabrics, enabling designers to manipulate them into three-dimensional shapes. Knife pleats, box pleats, and accordion pleats are just a few examples of pleating styles that can be employed to achieve different effects. By experimenting with the placement, size, and direction of pleats, designers can create intricate and eye-catching designs.

Ruching is another technique that can be used to create sculptural drapes. By gathering and stitching fabric at regular intervals, designers can create soft, flowing folds that add texture and movement to a garment. Ruching can be used strategically to highlight certain areas of a design or to create a more overall sculpted effect.

Gathering is a technique that involves drawing fabric together to create folds or gathers. This method can be used to create voluminous drapes or to add texture to specific areas of a design. When combined with pleating or ruching, gathering can create even more intricate and visually appealing effects.

Origami-inspired techniques can also be incorporated into structured design to create sculptural drapes and folds. By folding and manipulating fabric in a precise and calculated manner, designers can create geometric shapes and architectural details that give garments a futuristic and avant-garde feel.

In conclusion, creating sculptural drapes and folds is an essential skill for fashion designers working in the niche of structured design. By mastering techniques such as pleating, ruching, gathering, and origami-inspired folding, designers can elevate their designs to new heights. The use of these techniques adds depth, dimension, and drama to garments, creating statement pieces that capture attention and leave a lasting impression. With creativity and precision, fashion designers can transform simple designs into works of art that showcase their unique vision and expertise in structured couture.

Using Stiffening Agents for Structural Support

In the world of fashion design, structure plays a vital role in creating visually stunning and high-fashion garments. The ability to manipulate fabric and create unique silhouettes requires an understanding of various techniques and tools. One such technique is the use of stiffening agents for structural support.

Stiffening agents serve as a backbone for structured designs, providing stability and shape to garments. These agents can be in the form of interfacings, fusible tapes, or even certain types of fabrics. They are strategically placed in areas that require reinforcement, such as collars, cuffs, and hems, to ensure they maintain their intended shape.

Interfacings, commonly made of woven or non-woven materials, are the most commonly used stiffening agents in fashion design. They are applied to the wrong side of the fabric, either through sewing or fusing, to add rigidity and support. Fusible tapes, on the other hand, are narrow strips of adhesive material that can be applied directly to fabric edges to prevent fraying and add structure.

When selecting a stiffening agent, it is crucial to consider the desired outcome of the garment. Different agents provide varying degrees of stiffness, and choosing the right one is essential to achieve the desired effect. Additionally, the weight, drape, and texture of the fabric being used should also be taken into account to ensure the stiffening agent complements the overall design.

Experimentation and practice are key when using stiffening agents for structural support. Fashion designers must familiarize themselves with different types of interfacings and their effects on various fabrics.

Understanding how the fabric reacts to the stiffening agent is crucial to avoid any unwanted stiffness or distortion.

By mastering the art of using stiffening agents, fashion designers can push the boundaries of structured design. They can create garments that defy gravity and captivate audiences with their intricate and visually stunning silhouettes. From architectural-inspired dresses to sculptural collars, the possibilities are endless when it comes to incorporating structure into fashion design.

In conclusion, the use of stiffening agents for structural support is a fundamental technique in structured design for fashion. It allows fashion designers to create garments that stand out from the crowd and showcase their creativity and precision. With the right selection of stiffening agents and a keen eye for detail, fashion designers can transform their visions into reality, bringing their high-fashion designs to life.

Chapter 5: Techniques for Precision in Construction

Mastering Tailoring Techniques for Structured Couture

In the world of fashion design, mastering the art of tailoring techniques is essential for creating stunning structured couture pieces. From precise measurements to impeccable construction, every detail plays a vital role in achieving high-fashion designs that exude precision and elegance. This subchapter aims to provide fashion designers specialized in structured design with a comprehensive guide to mastering tailoring techniques.

One of the fundamental aspects of mastering tailoring techniques is understanding the importance of precise measurements. Accurate measuring ensures that your garment fits flawlessly on the wearer's body, enhancing their silhouette and creating a stunning visual impact. From the bust to the hips and waist, every measurement should be meticulously taken to achieve optimal fit and structure.

Once the measurements are acquired, it is crucial to translate them into precise pattern drafting and cutting. This subchapter will delve into the intricacies of pattern-making for structured couture, providing step-by-step instructions and tips to create well-fitted and visually appealing garments. From darts and pleats to princess seams and tailored collars, each element contributes to the desired structured effect.

Sewing techniques play a significant role in achieving a refined and polished finished product. This subchapter will explore various advanced sewing techniques such as hand-stitching, understitching, and the art of creating perfectly aligned seams. Additionally, it will cover techniques like boning, interlining, and interfacing to add structure and support to the garment.

To elevate your structured couture designs, attention to detail is paramount. This subchapter will guide you through the art of precision pressing, fabric manipulation, and topstitching techniques. These techniques will add depth and dimension to your creations, creating a visually stunning and impeccably tailored result.

Finally, this subchapter will discuss the importance of practicing patience and perseverance in mastering tailoring techniques. It takes time and dedication to hone your skills, but the end result is well worth the effort. Through practice and continuous learning, you can refine your craftsmanship and create exceptional structured couture designs that stand out in the world of fashion.

In conclusion, mastering tailoring techniques is a crucial aspect of creating high-fashion designs with precision. This subchapter provides fashion designers specializing in structured design with a comprehensive guide to mastering the art of tailoring. By understanding the significance of precise measurements, pattern-making, sewing techniques, attention to detail, and practicing perseverance, you can create stunning structured couture pieces that leave a lasting impression.

Precision Stitching and Finishing Methods

In the world of fashion design, attention to detail is paramount. One wrong stitch or sloppy finish can ruin an otherwise impeccable garment. For those who specialize in structured design for fashion, precision stitching and finishing methods are essential skills to master. These techniques not only ensure a flawless finish but also contribute to the longevity and durability of the garment.

Precision stitching involves using the right tools, techniques, and materials to create clean, even, and secure stitches. One of the most commonly used methods is machine stitching, which allows for consistent and accurate results. However, hand stitching should not be overlooked, especially for intricate details or delicate fabrics. Both techniques require a steady hand, patience, and a keen eye for detail.

Choosing the appropriate thread for each project is crucial. The weight, color, and fiber content of the thread should complement the fabric and design. For example, a heavy-duty thread is ideal for structural seams, while a finer thread may be used for delicate details. Color matching is essential to maintain a cohesive look, ensuring that stitches seamlessly blend into the fabric.

Finishing methods are the final touches that elevate a garment from ordinary to extraordinary. One such technique is the use of binding, which provides a clean and professional edge to raw seams. Binding can be made from self-fabric or contrasting fabric, adding a touch of visual interest to the design.

Other finishing methods include French seams, which enclose raw edges for a neat and polished look, and topstitching, which adds decorative or functional elements. Precision pressing is also a vital step in finishing. Properly pressing seams and hems can make a significant difference in the overall appearance of the garment, ensuring crisp lines and a professional finish.

To achieve precision stitching and finishing, practicing on scraps and samples is essential. Experimenting with different techniques, fabrics, and threads will enhance your skills and expand your creative possibilities. Additionally, investing in quality tools, such as sharp scissors, fine needles, and reliable sewing machines, will contribute to consistent and accurate results.

In conclusion, precision stitching and finishing methods are fundamental skills for fashion designers specializing in structured designs. By mastering these techniques, designers can create high-fashion garments that are not only visually stunning but also durable and long-lasting. With attention to detail and a commitment to excellence, the possibilities for creating structured couture are endless.

Achieving Impeccable Fit and Proportions

In the world of fashion design, creating structured designs that exude elegance and sophistication requires meticulous attention to fit and proportions. The way a garment sits on the body can make or break its overall aesthetic appeal. To achieve impeccable fit and proportions, designers must combine precision, craftsmanship, and an understanding of the human form.

Fit is the foundation of any well-designed garment. It is essential to understand the different body types and measurements to tailor the design accordingly. Each individual has unique proportions, and it is the designer's task to flatter and enhance those natural curves. Taking accurate measurements and making precise adjustments is crucial to achieving a perfect fit.

One of the key elements in achieving impeccable fit is understanding garment construction and patternmaking. Structured designs rely on precise cutting, draping, and fitting techniques. The interplay between fabric, seams, and darts can create a sculptural effect, accentuating the desired silhouette. By using quality materials and paying attention to the smallest details, designers can elevate their creations to the realm of high fashion.

Proportions play a significant role in creating a visually appealing design. Understanding the relationship between different elements of a garment, such as the neckline, waistline, and hemline, is crucial in achieving a balanced composition. The designer must consider the wearer's body shape, height, and personal style to determine the ideal proportions for each design. Through careful experimentation and a keen eye for aesthetics, designers can create garments that flatter the body and create a harmonious overall look.

The use of structured design techniques allows designers to manipulate and mold the fabric to achieve their desired shape and form. Incorporating techniques such as boning, draping, and corsetry can create a stunningly tailored look. These techniques not only enhance the fit and proportions but also add an element of uniqueness and craftsmanship to the design.

Ultimately, achieving impeccable fit and proportions requires a deep understanding of the human body, a mastery of garment construction techniques, and an unwavering commitment to precision. By combining these elements, fashion designers specializing in structured designs can create masterful pieces that exude confidence, sophistication, and timeless elegance.

Handling Structural Challenges in Construction

In the world of fashion design, creating structured designs requires a deep understanding of construction techniques. From corsets to tailored suits, the ability to handle structural challenges is essential in bringing high-fashion designs to life. This subchapter will explore the various challenges that fashion designers face in constructing structured garments and provide practical tips on how to overcome them.

One of the most common challenges is achieving the desired shape and silhouette. Structural designs often require precise measurements and intricate pattern making to ensure a flawless fit. Fashion designers must possess a keen eye for detail and be well-versed in the principles of garment construction. Understanding how different fabrics drape and interact with the body is crucial in achieving the desired structural effect.

Another significant challenge is selecting the appropriate materials. Structured designs often demand sturdy fabrics that can hold their shape, such as heavy-weight silks, brocades, or even industrial materials like boning or wire. Designers must carefully consider the functionality, aesthetics, and comfort of the chosen materials to ensure that they complement the overall design.

The construction process itself can pose challenges, especially when it involves complex techniques like boning, padding, or interfacing. These techniques require precision and patience, as well as a solid understanding of garment construction. Fashion designers must be aware of the potential pitfalls and develop strategies to overcome them, such as using specialized tools or seeking expert advice.

In addition to these technical challenges, fashion designers also need to consider the practical aspects of wearable structured designs. Ensuring ease of movement, comfort, and durability are essential for creating garments that are not only visually stunning but also functional. Designers must strike a delicate balance between artistry and wearability, pushing the boundaries of structured design while ensuring that the garments can be comfortably worn by their clients.

To overcome these challenges, fashion designers can engage in continuous learning and experimentation. Studying the works of influential designers who have successfully tackled structural challenges can offer valuable insights and inspiration. Collaborating with skilled pattern makers, seamstresses, and tailors can also help overcome technical hurdles and achieve the desired results.

In conclusion, handling structural challenges in construction is a vital aspect of fashion design, especially in the niche of structured design. This subchapter has explored various challenges designers may encounter and provided practical tips to overcome them. By mastering the techniques, understanding fabric behavior, and considering practicality, fashion designers can create high-fashion designs with precision and finesse, making a lasting impact in the world of structured design for fashion.

Chapter 6: Enhancing Structured Designs with Details

Embellishments and Trims for Structured Couture

In the world of fashion design, structured couture is a niche that demands precision and attention to detail. Creating high-fashion designs with a structured silhouette requires not only a keen eye for shape and form but also an understanding of how to enhance these elements with the right embellishments and trims.

Embellishments play a crucial role in adding depth and visual interest to structured designs. From intricate beadwork to delicate embroidery, these embellishments can transform a garment from ordinary to extraordinary. When working with structured couture, it is essential to choose embellishments that complement the silhouette and enhance its architectural qualities. For example, a structured bodice with clean lines and sharp angles could benefit from geometric beadwork or metallic trims that accentuate its sleekness.

Trims, on the other hand, serve both a functional and decorative purpose in structured couture. They can be used to define edges, add structure, or create interesting details. When selecting trims for structured designs, it is important to consider the weight and texture of the fabric. For heavier fabrics like wool or brocade, trims such as braids or ribbons can add a touch of opulence and reinforce the garment's structure. On lighter fabrics like silk or chiffon, delicate lace trims or organza ribbons can lend a softness and femininity to the design.

One must also consider the placement of embellishments and trims to achieve a balanced and cohesive look. Strategic placement can highlight the garment's architectural features, draw attention to specific areas, or create a focal point. For instance, placing a row of delicate lace trim along the neckline of a structured dress can draw attention to the wearer's face, while carefully positioned beadwork can emphasize the curves and lines of a tailored jacket.

In this subchapter, we will delve into the world of embellishments and trims for structured couture, exploring various techniques, materials, and design considerations. We will provide inspiration and guidance to fashion designers looking to elevate their structured designs with the right embellishments and trims. Whether you are a seasoned designer or a student exploring the world of structured design, this subchapter will equip you with the knowledge and creativity to create stunning high-fashion designs that exude precision and elegance.

Incorporating Structural Accessories

When it comes to creating high-fashion designs with precision, one aspect that cannot be overlooked is the incorporation of structural accessories. These accessories not only add a unique and distinctive touch to your designs but also play a crucial role in enhancing the overall structure and silhouette of the garments.

Structural accessories can include a wide range of elements, such as boning, corsets, padding, and various types of undergarments. These accessories are essential in creating the desired shape and form for structured designs in fashion.

One of the most commonly used structural accessories is boning. Boning is typically made from materials like steel or plastic and is inserted into the seams or channels of a garment. It provides stability and structure, helping to create a defined shape and support the fabric. Boning is often used in corsets, bodices, and fitted dresses to create a sleek and structured silhouette.

Corsets, another popular structural accessory, have been a staple in fashion design for centuries. They are designed to cinch the waist and create an hourglass figure. Corsets can be made from various materials, such as satin, leather, or even metal, and are often adorned with intricate details like lace or embroidery. Incorporating a corset into a structured design not only adds visual interest but also helps in shaping the overall silhouette of the garment.

Padding is another essential structural accessory that can be used to create volume and shape in specific areas of a garment. Whether it's adding volume to the hips or creating a pronounced shoulder line, padding allows designers to manipulate the shape and form of their designs. It can be made from various materials like foam, cotton, or even specialized padding materials.

Undergarments, such as petticoats or crinolines, are also vital in achieving a structured design. These accessories are used to add volume and support to skirts and dresses, creating a dramatic and structured silhouette. Petticoats are typically made from layers of stiff fabric or netting, while crinolines are made from a more structured material like horsehair.

Incorporating structural accessories into your fashion designs not only adds a touch of sophistication and elegance but also allows you to create unique and eye-catching silhouettes. Whether it's using boning, corsets, padding, or undergarments, these accessories play a crucial role in achieving precision and structure in your designs.

As a fashion designer specializing in structured designs, mastering the art of incorporating structural accessories is essential. By understanding how these accessories work and experimenting with different techniques, you can elevate your designs to new heights and create truly remarkable pieces of structured couture.

Experimenting with Textures and Surfaces

In the world of fashion design, the use of textures and surfaces is a powerful tool that can elevate any design from ordinary to extraordinary. This subchapter titled "Experimenting with Textures and Surfaces" from our book "Structured Couture: Creating High-Fashion Designs with Precision" is dedicated to helping fashion designers in the niche of structured design explore the endless possibilities that textures and surfaces offer.

Textures and surfaces play a vital role in structured fashion design, as they can add depth, dimension, and visual interest to any garment. By experimenting with different textures and surfaces, designers can create unique and eye-catching designs that stand out in the fashion industry.

One way to experiment with textures is by incorporating various fabrics into a design. Mixing fabrics with different textures, such as silk, lace, leather, or velvet, can create a visually captivating contrast that adds a touch of luxury and sophistication to your designs. Furthermore, manipulating fabrics through techniques like pleating, ruffling, or gathering can create interesting textures that add movement and dynamism to your garments.

Another way to experiment with surfaces is by embellishing your designs with different materials and techniques. Embroidery, beading, sequins, or appliques can transform a plain fabric into a work of art. These surface embellishments not only add visual interest but can also create a tactile experience for the wearer and the viewer.

Additionally, designers can experiment with innovative surface treatments such as laser cutting, 3D printing, or heat bonding to create unique textures and patterns in their structured designs. These techniques allow for precise and intricate detailing, giving designers the freedom to push the boundaries of traditional fashion design.

Experimenting with textures and surfaces also involves understanding the relationship between the fabric and the structure of a garment. By strategically placing textured fabrics in areas that require volume or support, designers can enhance the overall silhouette and create a cohesive look that is both visually stunning and structurally sound.

In conclusion, the subchapter "Experimenting with Textures and Surfaces" in "Structured Couture: Creating High-Fashion Designs with Precision" aims to inspire and guide fashion designers in the niche of structured design. By exploring various textures, surfaces, and their manipulation techniques, designers can create truly extraordinary and unique garments that will make a lasting impact in the world of fashion. So, let your creativity soar and experiment with textures and surfaces to create high-fashion designs that are both visually captivating and structurally impressive.

Balancing Structure and Embellishment

In the realm of fashion design, the art of creating structured designs holds a prominent place. It involves meticulously crafting garments that not only exude elegance and sophistication but also possess a precise and well-defined structure. This subchapter, "Balancing Structure and Embellishment," from the book "Structured Couture: Creating High-Fashion Designs with Precision," serves as a guide for fashion designers seeking to master the art of structured design.

Creating structured designs requires a delicate balance between the foundation of the garment and the embellishments that adorn it. The structure provides the backbone and shape, while the embellishments add personality, flair, and uniqueness to the design. Achieving this balance is an art form that requires skill, knowledge, and a keen eye for detail.

One of the key elements discussed in this subchapter is the importance of understanding the principles of garment construction. Fashion designers must have a strong foundation in pattern-making, draping, and sewing techniques to create well-structured designs. By understanding how different fabrics drape and behave, designers can manipulate them to achieve the desired structural effect. The subchapter provides practical tips and techniques for achieving structural perfection, such as using boning, interlining, and strategic dart placement.

Embellishments play a crucial role in adding interest and enhancing the overall impact of structured designs. However, it is essential to strike a balance between embellishments and the underlying structure. Too many embellishments can overwhelm the design, while too little can render it dull and lacking in personality. This subchapter delves into the art of embellishment, discussing various techniques such as beading, embroidery, appliqué, and fabric manipulation. It also explores how designers can use embellishments to highlight and complement the structural elements of their designs.

Throughout the subchapter, "Balancing Structure and Embellishment," numerous examples and case studies from renowned fashion designers are provided. These real-life examples showcase the successful fusion of structure and embellishment, inspiring readers to experiment and push boundaries in their own designs.

For aspiring fashion designers and those in the niche of structured design, this subchapter serves as a valuable resource. It not only provides in-depth knowledge and practical techniques but also encourages designers to embrace the harmonious coexistence of structure and embellishment in their high-fashion creations. With the guidance offered in this subchapter, designers can master the art of balancing structure and embellishment, and create awe-inspiring designs that captivate the fashion world.

Chapter 7: Exploring Contemporary Structured Couture

Iconic Designers in Structured Fashion

In the world of fashion design, certain individuals have left an indelible mark on the industry with their innovative and groundbreaking creations. These iconic designers have mastered the art of structured fashion, pushing boundaries and redefining what is possible in the realm of high-fashion designs. In this subchapter, we delve into the lives and works of some of the most influential figures in the field of structured design for fashion, inspiring aspiring fashion designers to explore new horizons.

One of the most prominent names in structured fashion is Cristóbal Balenciaga. Known as the "master of haute couture," Balenciaga revolutionized the industry with his architectural silhouettes and meticulous attention to detail. His designs featured sculptural shapes, exaggerated volumes, and immaculate tailoring, captivating the fashion world and setting new standards for structured fashion.

Another trailblazer in the realm of structured design is Alexander McQueen. Renowned for his avant-garde and provocative creations, McQueen combined traditional tailoring techniques with innovative materials to create visually stunning garments. His ability to fuse structure and fantasy resulted in iconic pieces that challenged conventional notions of fashion.

The subchapter also highlights the contributions of Phoebe Philo, former creative director of Céline. Philo's minimalist approach to structured fashion brought a new level of sophistication to the industry. Her clean lines, precise cuts, and focus on functionality resonated with women worldwide, earning her acclaim as one of the most influential designers of her generation.

Additionally, the subchapter explores the work of Rei Kawakubo, the visionary behind the fashion label Comme des Garçons. Kawakubo's designs defy categorization, often blurring the lines between fashion and art. Her avant-garde creations challenge conventional notions of structure, with asymmetrical cuts, unconventional fabric combinations, and deconstructed silhouettes becoming her signature.

By studying the works of these iconic designers, fashion enthusiasts can gain valuable insights into the world of structured fashion design. Understanding their creative processes, attention to detail, and willingness to break boundaries can inspire and empower emerging fashion designers to experiment with structure, precision, and innovation in their own designs.

Structured Couture: Creating High-Fashion Designs with Precision serves as a comprehensive guide for fashion designers interested in exploring the niche of structured design. By analyzing the works of these iconic designers and showcasing their contributions to the field, the book aims to encourage readers to push their creative boundaries, master the art of structure, and create designs that will leave a lasting impact on the world of fashion.

Modern Innovations in Structured Design

Subchapter: Modern Innovations in Structured Design

Introduction:

In the ever-evolving world of fashion, structured design has always held a special place. It is a technique that seamlessly combines precision, functionality, and aesthetic appeal. With the rise of technology and the advent of innovative materials, the possibilities for structured design in fashion have expanded exponentially. This subchapter delves into the exciting modern innovations that have revolutionized structured design and opened up new avenues for fashion designers to create high-fashion designs with unparalleled precision.

1. Advanced Fabrication Techniques:

One of the most notable advancements in structured design is the development of advanced fabrication techniques. These techniques utilize cutting-edge technologies such as 3D printing, laser cutting, and computerized pattern-making to create intricately structured garments. Fashion designers can experiment with complex geometric patterns, innovative draping techniques, and custom-fit designs, resulting in garments that are not only visually stunning but also perfectly tailored to the wearer's body.

2. Smart Materials:

Another game-changer in structured design is the emergence of smart materials. These materials have built-in properties that respond to environmental factors, such as temperature, light, or moisture. For example, shape-memory fabrics can be used to create garments that can change shape or adapt to the wearer's body over time. Self-repairing materials can mend small damages, increasing the longevity of structured garments. These smart materials not only enhance the functionality and durability of structured designs but also add an element of intrigue and innovation to the fashion world.

3. Sustainable Structured Design:

As the fashion industry embraces sustainability, structured design has also evolved to meet this growing demand. Designers are now exploring eco-friendly materials, such as recycled plastics or organic textiles, to create structured garments that are both stylish and environmentally conscious. Additionally, the use of zero-waste pattern-making techniques ensures that every piece of fabric is utilized, minimizing waste and reducing the ecological footprint of structured fashion designs.

4. Virtual Prototyping and Augmented Reality:

Advancements in virtual prototyping and augmented reality have transformed the design process for structured garments. Fashion designers can now create virtual simulations of their designs, allowing them to visualize and refine the structure before producing physical prototypes. Augmented reality tools enable designers to virtually drape garments on models or display the inner workings of structured designs, providing a deeper understanding of the construction process.

Conclusion:

The modern innovations in structured design have redefined the possibilities for fashion designers. With advanced fabrication techniques, smart materials, sustainable practices, and virtual prototyping tools, the world of structured fashion design is more exciting and dynamic than ever before. As fashion designers embrace these innovations, they can create high-fashion designs with precision and ingenuity, pushing the boundaries of structured design and captivating audiences with their creations. Structured Couture is at the forefront of this revolution, empowering designers to unleash their creativity and create fashion that is both visually striking and technically impeccable.

Pushing Boundaries with Avant-Garde Structures

Avant-garde structures have long been at the forefront of fashion design, challenging conventional notions of form and pushing the boundaries of what is considered wearable art. In the realm of structured design for fashion, avant-garde structures offer a unique opportunity to create innovative and captivating high-fashion designs that resonate with the bold and daring.

This subchapter delves into the world of avant-garde structures, exploring the techniques, inspirations, and possibilities they offer to fashion designers looking to create truly exceptional and boundary-pushing designs.

Avant-garde structures in fashion are characterized by their unconventional shapes, architectural elements, and experimental materials. These structures often defy traditional garment construction techniques, embracing asymmetry, exaggerated silhouettes, and unexpected combinations of fabrics to create visually striking and thought-provoking designs.

One of the key techniques used in avant-garde structures is draping. By skillfully manipulating fabric, fashion designers can create voluminous shapes, unusual proportions, and dynamic folds that challenge the notion of what a garment should look like. Draping allows for the creation of sculptural forms that interact with the body in unexpected ways, blurring the lines between fashion and fine art.

Another technique commonly employed in avant-garde structures is the use of unconventional materials. Designers may experiment with materials such as metal, wire, plastic, or even unconventional textiles to create garments that embody a sense of innovation and boundary-pushing. The juxtaposition of different textures and materials adds depth and interest to the overall design, capturing the attention of fashion enthusiasts and industry insiders alike.

Avant-garde structures draw inspiration from a variety of sources, including architecture, nature, and technology. The fusion of these influences results in designs that are both futuristic and organic, challenging preconceived notions of what is considered fashionable. From the fluid lines of a futuristic skyscraper to the intricate patterns found in nature, avant-garde structures offer endless possibilities for fashion designers to create truly unique and awe-inspiring pieces.

Ultimately, avant-garde structures in fashion design offer a platform for self-expression and creative exploration. They encourage designers to think outside the box, to question conventional norms, and to push the boundaries of what is possible in the realm of structured couture. By embracing avant-garde structures, fashion designers have the opportunity to leave a lasting impact on the industry, creating designs that captivate and inspire the fashion world for years to come.

In conclusion, the subchapter "Pushing Boundaries with Avant-Garde Structures" explores the world of avant-garde structures in fashion design, emphasizing their unique techniques, inspirations, and possibilities. By embracing these bold and daring structures, fashion designers can create high-fashion designs with precision, pushing the boundaries of structured couture and leaving a lasting impact on the industry.

Balancing Tradition and Innovation in Structured Couture

In the world of fashion design, where trends come and go at lightning speed, finding the perfect balance between tradition and innovation is crucial. This is particularly true when it comes to structured couture, a niche that demands precision and attention to detail. In this subchapter, we will explore how designers can navigate the delicate dance between tradition and innovation to create high-fashion designs that stand the test of time.

Tradition forms the backbone of structured couture. It encompasses the techniques, craftsmanship, and design principles that have been passed down through generations. These traditions provide a solid foundation for designers to build upon, ensuring that their creations possess a timeless quality. From meticulously tailored corsets to intricate pleating and draping techniques, traditional methods offer a sense of elegance and sophistication that cannot be replicated.

However, in order to keep up with the ever-evolving fashion landscape, designers must also embrace innovation. This entails pushing the boundaries of what is considered traditional and exploring new techniques, materials, and technologies. By infusing their designs with innovative elements, designers can breathe new life into structured couture, making it relevant and compelling for contemporary audiences.

One way to strike a balance between tradition and innovation is to reinterpret classic silhouettes with modern twists. For instance, a traditional ball gown can be reinvented with unconventional fabrics or unexpected embellishments, injecting a fresh perspective into a timeless design. This fusion of old and new creates a captivating juxtaposition that appeals to both traditionalists and avant-garde fashion enthusiasts.

Furthermore, embracing innovation in the construction process can enhance the functionality and durability of structured couture. Incorporating technologies such as 3D printing and laser cutting allows designers to create intricate patterns and structural elements that were previously impossible or time-consuming to achieve. By harnessing these tools, designers can elevate their craftsmanship and create garments that are both visually stunning and structurally sound.

In conclusion, balancing tradition and innovation is essential in the realm of structured couture. By honoring and building upon traditional techniques while embracing innovation, designers can create high-fashion designs with precision that captivate audiences and withstand the test of time. The key lies in finding the delicate equilibrium between the two, resulting in garments that embody the best of both worlds and push the boundaries of what is considered possible in the world of fashion design.

Chapter 8: From Concept to Runway: The Creative Process

Developing a Concept for Structured Designs

In the world of fashion design, creating structured designs is a niche that requires precision, attention to detail, and a deep understanding of construction techniques. Structured designs are known for their clean lines, architectural shapes, and well-defined silhouettes. They represent a fusion of art and engineering, where the designer's creativity is combined with meticulous planning and execution.

To embark on the journey of developing structured designs, it is essential for fashion designers to have a clear concept in mind. A concept acts as a guiding force, providing a vision and direction for the design process. It sets the tone for the overall aesthetic and helps in making design decisions.

Before diving into the development of a concept, it is important to research and gather inspiration from various sources. This could include studying past structured designs, exploring architectural forms, examining nature's geometry, or even looking into other art forms. This research phase helps in broadening creative horizons and provides a foundation for the concept development.

Once the research phase is complete, the next step is to translate the gathered inspiration into a cohesive concept. This can be achieved by analyzing the key elements that define structured designs. Elements such as symmetry, clean lines, geometric shapes, and architectural influences should be considered while developing the concept.

A well-developed concept should not only reflect the designer's personal style but also resonate with their target audience. Understanding the preferences and expectations of the niche market for structured design is crucial in creating designs that are both unique and commercially viable.

The concept development process involves sketching, creating mood boards, and experimenting with different fabric swatches to visualize the desired aesthetic. It is essential to focus on the balance between form and function, ensuring that the structured design not only looks visually appealing but is also wearable and comfortable.

Once a solid concept is developed, it serves as a roadmap for the subsequent design stages, including pattern making, fabric selection, and garment construction. The concept helps in maintaining consistency and coherence throughout the design process, resulting in a well-executed structured design that meets both creative and technical standards.

In conclusion, developing a concept for structured designs is a crucial step in the world of fashion design. It sets the tone for the overall aesthetic, provides direction, and acts as a guiding force throughout the design process. By researching, gathering inspiration, and analyzing key elements, fashion designers can create unique and visually appealing structured designs that resonate with their target audience. With precision and attention to detail, structured designs can elevate fashion to a whole new level of artistry and craftsmanship.

Sketching and Storyboarding Structured Couture

In the world of fashion design, the ability to effectively communicate your ideas visually is just as important as the technical skills required to create the actual garments. Sketching and storyboarding are two essential techniques that allow fashion designers to bring their structured couture designs to life with precision and creativity.

Sketching is the initial step in the design process, where designers put their ideas onto paper. When it comes to structured design for fashion, sketching plays a crucial role in capturing the unique elements that define this niche. It allows designers to experiment with different shapes, silhouettes, and textures, ensuring that every detail is meticulously planned and executed.

To sketch structured couture garments, designers must understand the principles of proportion, balance, and construction. They need to convey the architectural elements of their designs through accurate and detailed renderings. By using various drawing techniques, such as shading and highlighting, designers can create depth and dimension on the flat surface of the paper, giving their sketches a three-dimensional feel.

Storyboarding is another technique that helps fashion designers visualize the progression of their designs. It involves creating a series of sketches that depict the different stages of a garment's development. For structured couture, storyboarding becomes even more critical, as it allows designers to plan and showcase the intricate construction techniques involved in creating these elaborate pieces.

Through storyboarding, designers can experiment with different compositions and arrangements of design elements. They can explore how various fabrics, embellishments, and structural elements work together to create a cohesive and stunning final piece. Storyboards also serve as a valuable tool for communication, enabling designers to present their ideas to clients, manufacturers, and other stakeholders involved in the production process.

In the subchapter "Sketching and Storyboarding Structured Couture," readers will delve into the world of structured design for fashion. They will learn the techniques required to sketch and storyboard intricate and precise couture garments. From mastering the basics of proportion and balance to creating detailed renderings that capture the essence of structured couture, this subchapter will provide fashion designers with the knowledge and skills they need to bring their creative visions to life.

By understanding the art of sketching and storyboarding, fashion designers can effectively communicate their ideas, allowing for a seamless transition from concept to realization. Whether you're a budding designer or an experienced professional seeking to enhance your skills in structured couture, this subchapter will serve as a valuable resource in your fashion design journey.

Planning and Executing the Design Process

In the world of fashion design, creating structured designs that stand out requires precision and meticulous planning. This subchapter will delve into the essential steps involved in planning and executing the design process for structured fashion designs. Whether you are a budding fashion designer or an experienced professional looking to enhance your skills in structured design, this subchapter will provide you with invaluable insights.

The first step in planning any structured design is thorough research. Get acquainted with the latest trends in structured fashion design by studying renowned designers and their collections. Analyze their use of structure, silhouette, and embellishments to understand how they create visually striking pieces. Additionally, explore the history of structured designs to gain inspiration and insight into classic techniques that can be reinterpreted in a contemporary context.

Once you have gathered sufficient inspiration, it's time to move on to the sketching phase. Sketching helps bring your ideas to life and allows you to experiment with various silhouettes, cut lines, and structural elements. Don't be afraid to push boundaries and explore unconventional shapes and proportions. This is your chance to let your creativity shine.

After finalizing your sketches, it's essential to create a detailed technical drawing. This drawing serves as a blueprint for your design and aids in accurately executing your vision. Include measurements, fabric details, and any other pertinent information that will guide you during the construction process.

Next, you will need to source materials and create a prototype. Select fabrics that complement your design and ensure they possess the necessary qualities to achieve the desired structure. When constructing the prototype, pay close attention to the precision of your cuts, seams, and finishes. This is the stage where your design truly starts to take shape.

Once the prototype is complete, be sure to conduct a thorough fitting session. Assess the fit, structure, and overall aesthetic of the garment. Make necessary adjustments to ensure optimum comfort and visual impact.

Finally, it's time to execute the final design. Take into account any modifications identified during the fitting session and meticulously construct the final garment. Pay attention to every detail, from stitching to embellishments, as they contribute to the overall quality and appeal of your design.

By following these steps, you will be well on your way to creating high-fashion structured designs with precision. Remember, planning and executing the design process is as crucial as the final result. So, embrace the journey, experiment fearlessly, and let your structured designs make a lasting impression in the world of fashion.

Presenting Structured Designs on the Runway

When it comes to showcasing structured designs on the runway, precision and meticulous craftsmanship are essential. Structured couture has become a prominent niche in the fashion design industry, with designers incorporating architectural elements into their creations. This subchapter will delve into the art of presenting these high-fashion designs with precision, capturing the attention of both the fashion industry and the audience.

The runway is the perfect platform to showcase the intricate details and skills involved in creating structured designs. It allows designers to bring their vision to life, highlighting the precision and artistry behind each piece. These designs often incorporate bold shapes, clean lines, and carefully constructed forms that accentuate the human figure.

One of the most crucial aspects of presenting structured designs on the runway is ensuring that the garments fit the models perfectly. Tailoring plays a vital role in achieving this, as it is essential to create pieces that flatter the wearer's body while maintaining the intended structure. Designers must pay close attention to measurements, ensuring that each garment is tailored to perfection.

Another aspect to consider is the choreography of the runway show. Structured designs often require models to move in a way that accentuates the garment's shape and structure. Choreographing the models' movements to showcase the design's unique features is crucial. This can include strategic poses, turns, and walks that highlight the architectural elements of the garment.

Lighting and staging also play a significant role in presenting structured designs effectively. Proper lighting can enhance the shadows and highlights of the garment, emphasizing its structure and creating a dramatic effect. Thoughtful staging can also help create a cohesive environment that complements the designs being presented.

To present structured designs successfully, it is essential to create a narrative that ties the collection together. Designers can choose a theme or concept that resonates with their vision and use it as a thread that connects each piece. This cohesive narrative adds depth and meaning to the collection, allowing the audience to engage with the designs on a deeper level.

In conclusion, presenting structured designs on the runway requires meticulous attention to detail, precision tailoring, thoughtful choreography, and strategic lighting and staging. These elements come together to create an immersive experience that showcases the artistry and craftsmanship behind each structured couture creation. By following these guidelines, fashion designers can captivate the audience, leaving a lasting impression and establishing themselves as masters of structured design in the industry.

Chapter 9: Marketing and Selling Structured Couture

Identifying the Target Market for Structured Designs

In the world of fashion design, understanding your target market is crucial for success. This is especially true when it comes to the niche of structured design. Structured couture, with its emphasis on precision and architectural silhouettes, appeals to a specific group of fashion enthusiasts who appreciate the artistry and craftsmanship behind these designs. In this subchapter, we will delve into the process of identifying the target market for structured designs and how to effectively cater to their needs.

The target market for structured designs primarily consists of fashion-forward individuals who are drawn to bold and avant-garde aesthetics. These individuals are often trendsetters, seeking unique and innovative designs that make a statement. They appreciate the meticulous attention to detail and the sculptural qualities that structured garments offer.

One key aspect of identifying the target market for structured designs is understanding their lifestyle and preferences. Structured couture is often associated with high-end events, such as red carpet occasions and luxury parties. Therefore, it is essential to consider the occasions and events that your target market attends, as well as their social circles and aspirations. By doing so, you can create designs that align with their lifestyle and cater to their specific needs.

Another important factor to consider when identifying the target market for structured designs is demographics. While structured couture can appeal to individuals of various ages, it typically attracts a slightly older demographic with a higher disposable income. These individuals value quality over quantity and are willing to invest in timeless pieces that will stand the test of time.

Understanding the psychographics of your target market is equally important. This involves delving into their personality traits, values, and motivations. Structured design enthusiasts tend to be confident, self-assured, and unafraid to make a bold fashion statement. They appreciate the artistry and craftsmanship behind structured designs, valuing originality and individuality.

To effectively cater to the target market for structured designs, it is crucial to conduct thorough market research. This can involve analyzing fashion trends, studying competitor brands, and engaging with potential customers through surveys or focus groups. By gaining insights into their preferences, you can tailor your designs to meet their expectations and desires.

In conclusion, identifying the target market for structured designs requires a deep understanding of their lifestyle, demographics, and psychographics. By catering to their needs and preferences, you can create high-fashion designs that resonate with this niche audience. Remember, precision and artistry are the cornerstones of structured couture, and by aligning your designs with the desires of your target market, you can carve a niche for yourself in the world of fashion design.

Branding and Positioning Your Structured Couture Line

In the world of fashion design, creating a unique and recognizable brand is crucial for success. This is especially true in the niche of structured design for fashion. Your structured couture line is a reflection of your creativity, precision, and attention to detail, and it is essential to effectively brand and position your line to stand out in the competitive fashion industry.

Branding is more than just a logo or a name. It encompasses the overall image and identity of your structured couture line. Start by defining the core values and aesthetic of your brand. What makes your designs unique? What story do you want to tell through your creations? These questions will guide you in building a strong brand identity.

Once you have established your brand, it is important to consistently communicate it through various channels. Create a visually captivating logo and ensure it is present on your website, social media profiles, and promotional materials. Use consistent colors, typography, and imagery to create a cohesive brand experience across all platforms.

Positioning your structured couture line involves identifying your target audience and understanding their needs and desires. Who is your ideal customer? Consider factors such as age, income, lifestyle, and fashion preferences. Conduct market research to gain insights into your target audience's buying patterns and trends. This will help you tailor your designs and marketing strategies to effectively reach and engage with your audience.

Differentiate your structured couture line by highlighting its unique selling points. Is it the intricate construction techniques, impeccable fit, or use of sustainable materials? Whatever sets your line apart from others, emphasize it in your branding and marketing efforts. Showcase your craftsmanship through high-quality photographs and detailed descriptions of your designs.

Collaborations with influencers, stylists, and fashion bloggers can also help position your structured couture line in the industry. Seek out partnerships that align with your brand values and aesthetics, as these collaborations will expose your line to a wider audience and enhance its credibility.

Finally, engage with your audience through social media, fashion shows, and events. Create a community around your structured couture line by sharing behind-the-scenes footage, design inspirations, and customer testimonials. Encourage feedback and actively listen to your customers' opinions to continuously refine and improve your brand.

In conclusion, branding and positioning your structured couture line require careful consideration and strategic planning. By defining your brand identity, effectively communicating it, understanding your target audience, and highlighting your unique selling points, you can successfully position your line in the competitive world of fashion design.

Pricing Strategies for High-Fashion Structured Pieces

When it comes to high-fashion structured pieces, pricing plays a crucial role in determining the perceived value of the design. As a fashion designer specializing in structured designs, it is important to understand the various pricing strategies that can be applied to ensure profitability and market success. In this subchapter, we will delve into the key considerations and strategies for pricing your high-fashion structured pieces effectively.

One of the primary factors to consider when determining the price of a structured design is the quality of materials used. High-fashion structured pieces often rely on luxurious fabrics, intricate embellishments, and meticulous craftsmanship. These premium materials significantly contribute to the overall cost of production and justify a higher price point. However, it is important to strike a balance between quality and affordability, ensuring that the price is reasonable enough for your target audience.

Another important consideration is the exclusivity and uniqueness of your design. High-fashion structured pieces are often sought after by fashion enthusiasts who appreciate one-of-a-kind creations. By incorporating unique design elements, limited edition releases, or even collaboration with other designers, you can create a sense of exclusivity and justify a higher price tag.

Market research is essential to understanding the pricing landscape in the world of structured fashion design. Analyze your competitors, their pricing strategies, and their target audience. This will help you position your brand and price your designs accordingly. Consider the demand for structured pieces in the market and adjust your pricing strategy accordingly, ensuring that you offer a competitive edge.

Promotional pricing strategies can also be effective in generating interest and boosting sales for high-fashion structured pieces. Limited-time discounts, flash sales, or bundle offers can create a sense of urgency and encourage customers to make a purchase. However, it is important to maintain the perceived value of your brand and not devalue your designs through excessive discounting.

Lastly, consider the pricing structure for different distribution channels. If you plan to sell your structured pieces through high-end boutiques or luxury department stores, the price may need to be higher to cover the markups and commissions. On the other hand, if you opt for direct-to-consumer sales through your website or pop-up shops, you may have more flexibility in setting the pricing.

In conclusion, pricing high-fashion structured pieces requires careful consideration of factors such as material quality, exclusivity, market research, promotional strategies, and distribution channels. By employing these strategies effectively, you can ensure that your designs are priced appropriately, maximizing profitability while appealing to your target audience of fashion design and structured design enthusiasts.

Retailing and Promoting Structured Couture Collections

In the fast-paced world of fashion design, staying ahead of the curve is critical to success. As a designer working in the niche of structured design for fashion, it is essential to understand how to effectively retail and promote your couture collections. This subchapter will delve into the various strategies and tactics you can employ to showcase your structured couture creations and reach your target audience.

1. Creating a Compelling Brand Image: Building a strong brand image is crucial in the competitive fashion industry. Develop a unique brand identity that reflects your structured design aesthetic. Consider factors such as your logo, color schemes, and overall brand positioning. Consistency is key, both online and offline.

2. Engaging in Strategic Marketing: Identify your target market and understand their preferences. Craft marketing campaigns that resonate with your audience. Utilize both traditional and digital marketing channels to create buzz around your structured couture collections. Collaborate with influencers, fashion bloggers, and stylists to promote your designs to a wider audience.

3. Showcasing at Fashion Weeks and Events: Participating in prestigious fashion weeks and industry events is an excellent opportunity to gain exposure. Secure a spot in fashion shows or organize your own runway event to showcase your structured couture collections. This allows potential buyers, industry professionals, and fashion enthusiasts to experience your creations firsthand.

4. Building Relationships with Retailers and Buyers: Developing strong relationships with retailers and buyers is crucial for the success of your structured couture business. Attend trade shows and fashion markets to connect with potential stockists and buyers. Create lookbooks and line sheets that highlight your collections and their unique selling points. Offer personalized assistance and incentives to retailers to encourage them to carry your designs.

5. Leveraging Online Platforms: In today's digital age, having a strong online presence is essential. Create a visually stunning website that showcases your structured couture collections. Utilize social media platforms to engage with your audience, share behind-the-scenes content, and announce new launches. Consider selling your designs through e-commerce platforms to reach a global customer base.

6. Providing Exceptional Customer Service: Deliver exceptional customer service to build brand loyalty. Provide personalized assistance to clients, offer alterations, and ensure timely delivery of orders. Encourage satisfied customers to share their experiences and reviews, which can serve as powerful testimonials for your structured couture brand.

By implementing these strategies and approaches, you can effectively retail and promote your structured couture collections. Remember, success in the fashion industry requires a combination of creativity, business acumen, and a deep understanding of your target audience. Stay true to your unique design aesthetic and consistently strive for excellence in all aspects of your business.

Chapter 10: The Future of Structured Couture

Trends and Innovations in Structured Design

In the fast-paced world of fashion design, staying ahead of the curve is essential. As the industry continues to evolve, so does the art of structured design. This subchapter delves into the latest trends and innovations in structured design for fashion, providing valuable insights and inspiration for aspiring fashion designers.

One of the most prominent trends in structured design is the fusion of traditional techniques with modern technologies. Designers are embracing the use of 3D printing, laser cutting, and digital modeling to create intricate and precise structural elements. These technologies allow for greater experimentation and customization, pushing the boundaries of what is possible in structured design.

Another exciting trend is the incorporation of sustainable materials and practices in structured design. With growing concerns about the environmental impact of the fashion industry, designers are seeking eco-friendly alternatives. This includes the use of recycled materials, organic fabrics, and innovative sustainable technologies. Structured design can now be environmentally conscious, without sacrificing style or quality.

In terms of silhouettes, there is a resurgence of bold and exaggerated shapes in structured design. Oversized shoulders, voluminous skirts, and architectural details are making a statement on runways and in high-end boutiques. Designers are playing with proportions and geometry, creating visually striking pieces that grab attention and celebrate individuality.

Innovations in structured design are not limited to garments alone; they extend to accessories as well. Structured handbags, shoes, and jewelry are becoming increasingly popular, adding an extra layer of sophistication and uniqueness to overall fashion ensembles. These accessories often feature intricate structural elements, such as geometric cutouts and metal frameworks, showcasing the designer's attention to detail and craftsmanship.

Lastly, the integration of technology into structured design is revolutionizing the industry. Wearable technology, such as embedded sensors and LED lights, are being seamlessly incorporated into structured garments, enhancing functionality and aesthetics. These innovative designs blur the lines between fashion and technology, creating exciting possibilities for the future of structured design.

As fashion design continues to evolve, structured design remains a timeless and essential element. By embracing the latest trends and innovations, aspiring fashion designers specializing in structured design can create high-fashion designs with precision and style. This subchapter serves as a guide, inspiring creativity and encouraging designers to push the boundaries of structured design to new heights.

Sustainability and Ethics in Structured Fashion

In the ever-evolving world of fashion design, the concept of sustainability and ethics has gained significant importance. As designers, it is crucial for us to consider the environmental and social impact of our creations, especially when it comes to structured designs in fashion.

Structured fashion design, characterized by precise tailoring and architectural silhouettes, requires a meticulous approach that often involves the use of various materials, intricate stitching techniques, and complex construction methods. This level of craftsmanship and attention to detail is what sets structured designs apart, making them highly sought after in the fashion industry.

However, with great creativity comes great responsibility. The excessive use of resources, such as fabric waste, energy consumption, and chemical dyes, poses significant environmental challenges. As advocates for sustainable fashion, we need to explore ways to minimize our ecological footprint without compromising the precision and beauty of structured designs.

One approach to achieving sustainability in structured fashion is through the use of eco-friendly materials. Designers can opt for organic and recycled fabrics, which not only reduce the demand for new resources but also minimize the release of harmful chemicals into the environment. Additionally, incorporating sustainable techniques like zero-waste cutting or upcycling can help reduce fabric waste and promote a circular economy within the fashion industry.

Ethics also play a crucial role in structured fashion design. It is essential to consider the social impact of our creations, ensuring fair labor practices and safe working conditions throughout the supply chain. Collaborating with artisans and skilled craftsmen who uphold traditional techniques can not only preserve cultural heritage but also support local communities.

Furthermore, embracing inclusivity and diversity in structured fashion is essential for ethical design. By designing for people of all shapes, sizes, and backgrounds, we can challenge the prevailing standards of beauty and promote body positivity. This approach not only fosters a more inclusive industry but also encourages sustainable consumption by offering timeless designs that cater to a broader customer base.

As fashion designers specializing in structured designs, we have the power to transform the industry by integrating sustainability and ethics into our creative processes. By embracing eco-friendly materials, ethical production practices, and inclusive design principles, we can pave the way for a more responsible and conscious fashion future. Let us strive to create high-fashion structured designs with precision, while also making a positive impact on the world we live in.

Embracing Technology in Structured Couture

Technology has revolutionized every aspect of our lives, and the fashion industry is no exception. In the world of structured couture, where precision is key, the integration of technology has opened up a world of possibilities for fashion designers. From the initial design process to the production and presentation of high-fashion garments, embracing technology has become essential for those in the field of structured design.

One of the most significant advancements in technology for fashion design is the use of computer-aided design (CAD) software. CAD allows designers to create intricate and precise patterns, making it easier to experiment with different shapes and structures. With the help of CAD, designers can visualize their ideas and bring them to life with utmost precision. This not only saves time but also ensures that the final garment is flawlessly executed.

Another way technology has made its mark in structured couture is through the use of 3D printing. This innovative technique allows designers to create intricate and complex structures that were once impossible to achieve manually. With 3D printing, designers can experiment with unique textures, shapes, and materials, pushing the boundaries of traditional fashion design. It not only adds an element of surprise to the final product but also enables designers to create truly one-of-a-kind pieces.

Furthermore, the integration of technology in structured couture has paved the way for sustainable fashion practices. With the rise of eco-consciousness, designers are now using technology to create garments from recycled materials, reducing waste and minimizing the environmental impact. Through the use of advanced machinery and innovative techniques, fashion designers can transform discarded textiles into beautiful, structured couture pieces, showcasing the importance of sustainability in the industry.

The emergence of wearable technology has also influenced structured couture. Designers are incorporating smart textiles and interactive elements into their creations, blurring the line between fashion and technology. From garments that change color with the touch of a button to pieces that monitor the wearer's vital signs, the integration of technology has added an entirely new dimension to structured couture.

In conclusion, embracing technology in structured couture has revolutionized the fashion industry. With the help of CAD software, 3D printing, sustainable practices, and wearable technology, fashion designers can create intricate and precise garments that push the boundaries of traditional fashion design. As technology continues to evolve, it will undoubtedly play an even greater role in structured couture, allowing designers to create innovative, sustainable, and extraordinary pieces.

The Influence of Structured Couture on the Fashion Industry

Structured Couture has undoubtedly made a significant impact on the fashion industry, revolutionizing the way designers approach their craft. In this subchapter, we will explore the profound influence of structured design on the world of fashion and its relevance to the niche of fashion design.

Structured Couture refers to the meticulous process of creating high-fashion designs with precision, paying careful attention to the construction and tailoring of garments. This approach contrasts with the more fluid and relaxed nature of traditional couture, where draping and soft silhouettes often take center stage. By embracing structured design, fashion designers have brought a new level of sophistication and architectural beauty to the industry.

One of the key influences of structured couture is the emphasis it places on precise construction techniques. Fashion designers specializing in structured design must possess a deep understanding of pattern-making, tailoring, and garment construction. This focus on precision has elevated the overall quality and craftsmanship of fashion garments, resulting in impeccably fitted and visually striking pieces.

Moreover, structured couture has also influenced the way designers approach fabric selection. Fabrics with a firm hand, such as wool, silk organza, or neoprene, are favored for their ability to hold shape and create architectural forms. By carefully selecting and manipulating these materials, designers can create garments that defy gravity and showcase extraordinary volume and structure.

The influence of structured couture extends beyond the design process itself. It has permeated various aspects of the fashion industry, from runway shows to red carpet events. Structured designs have become synonymous with luxury and elegance, attracting the attention of celebrities, fashion influencers, and the media. The demand for structured couture garments has surged, driving the growth of specialized ateliers and haute couture houses.

For fashion designers specializing in structured design, this subchapter will serve as a guide to understanding the impact of their work on the broader fashion industry. By embracing structured couture techniques, designers can elevate their creations to new heights, standing out in a competitive market. Additionally, readers interested in the niche of structured design for fashion will gain invaluable insights into the intricacies of this specialized field.

In conclusion, the influence of structured couture on the fashion industry cannot be ignored. Its meticulous construction techniques, emphasis on precise tailoring, and architectural forms have revolutionized the way fashion designers approach their craft. By delving into the world of structured design, fashion designers and enthusiasts will gain a deeper appreciation for the artistry and innovation that this niche brings to the fashion industry.

Conclusion: Embracing Structure in Fashion Design

In the fast-paced and ever-changing world of fashion, there is a constant need for innovation and creativity. As fashion designers, we strive to create unique and captivating designs that not only showcase our artistic vision but also resonate with the masses. One approach that has gained significant prominence in recent years is structured design in fashion.

Throughout this book, "Structured Couture: Creating High-Fashion Designs with Precision," we have explored the concept of embracing structure in fashion design and its impact on the industry. We have delved into the techniques, principles, and inspirations that can elevate a design from ordinary to extraordinary.

The importance of structure in fashion design cannot be overstated. It provides the framework upon which we can build our creations, ensuring that they possess the necessary balance, proportion, and silhouette. Structure allows us to experiment with new materials, shapes, and forms, pushing the boundaries of what is considered conventional in the fashion world.

Structured design enables us to create garments that not only look visually stunning but also offer functionality and comfort. By carefully incorporating structural elements such as boning, corsetry, and architectural shapes, we can create garments that flatter the wearer's body and enhance their natural beauty.

Furthermore, embracing structure in fashion design opens up a world of possibilities for experimentation and innovation. By combining different materials, textures, and techniques, we can create garments that are visually striking and truly unique. Structure allows us to play with volume, layering, and sculptural elements, resulting in designs that leave a lasting impression.

The niche of structured design for fashion design offers countless opportunities for designers to make their mark in the industry. By mastering the art of structure, we can create high-fashion designs that not only captivate the runways but also find their way into the wardrobes of fashion enthusiasts worldwide.

In conclusion, the journey of embracing structure in fashion design is one that requires dedication, skill, and a keen eye for detail. By understanding the principles behind structured design and incorporating them into our creative process, we can create fashion that is not only visually stunning but also functional and innovative. So let us embrace structure and elevate our designs to new heights, inspiring the fashion world with precision and artistry.

Milton Keynes UK
Ingram Content Group UK Ltd.
UKHW020236221123
432980UK00016B/1228